THE CROW

A TRUE BOOK®

by

Christin Ditchfield

Children's Press®
A Division of Scholastic Inc.

New York Toronto London Auckland Sydney
Mexico City New Delhi Hong Kong
Danbury, Connecticut

A bear claw decoration

Content Consultant
Liz Sonneborn

The photograph on the title page shows a man wearing a headdress at the Crow Nation annual fair.

Library of Congress Cataloging-in-Publication Data
Ditchfield, Christin.
  The Crow / by Christin Ditchfield.
    p. cm. — (A true book)
  Includes bibliographical references and index.
  0-516-23645-8 (lib. bdg.)   0-516-25591-6 (pbk.)
  1. Crow Indians—Social life and customs—Juvenile literature. 2. Crow Indians—History—Juvenile literature. I. Title. II. Series.
E99.C92D58 2005
978.6004'975272—dc22   2004030508

CHILDREN'S PRESS, and A TRUE BOOK™, and associated logos are trademarks and/or registered trademarks of Scholastic Library Publishing. SCHOLASTIC and associated logos are trademarks and/or registered trademarks of Scholastic Inc.

7 8 9 10 R 14 13 12 11 10

Contents

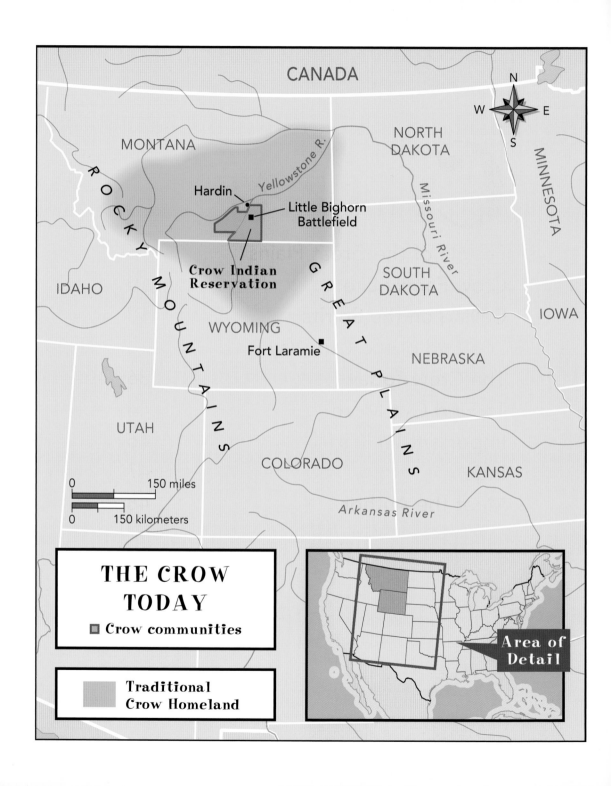

CANADA

MONTANA

NORTH DAKOTA

MINNESOTA

Yellowstone R.

Hardin

Little Bighorn Battlefield

Crow Indian Reservation

Missouri River

SOUTH DAKOTA

IOWA

R O C K Y   M O U N T A I N S

IDAHO

G R E A T   P L A I N S

WYOMING

Fort Laramie

NEBRASKA

UTAH

COLORADO

KANSAS

Arkansas River

0   150 miles

0   150 kilometers

THE CROW TODAY

☐ Crow communities

Area of Detail

Traditional Crow Homeland

People of the Great Plains

North America has been home to American Indians for many centuries. In the 1600s, about 500 members of one American Indian tribe, the Hidatsa, moved west into the Rocky Mountains along the Yellowstone River. The Hidatsa leader, No Vitals, had a vision in which he was told to search for the **sacred** tobacco plant. This plant was supposed to protect the people and give them **supernatural** power and strength. This vision led the people to what is now southern Montana and northern Wyoming.

The new tribe called itself *Apsaalooke*, which means "children of the long-beaked bird." Later, they became known as the Crow. For hundreds of years, the Hidatsa had raised

The Crow settled in southern Montana and northern Wyoming. The Bighorn Canyon National Recreation Area (above) is located in this area.

A Crow woman holds her baby while sitting on a buffalo hide inside a tepee.

their families in homes and villages that were part of larger farming communities. Now the Crow became buffalo hunters. They divided into bands, each made up of several families. Each band had about twenty to thirty people in all. They moved from place to place in search of food, herds of animals for hunting, and good weather.

Crow Family Life

For more than two hundred years, the Crow lived a **nomadic** life. They became skilled horsemen and expert hunters, as they followed the buffalo herds across the Great Plains. Crow men also hunted for deer, bear, elk, and bighorn sheep. The women

A herd of buffalo grazes in Wyoming.

gathered roots, berries, and herbs. These were used in soups and stews.

The Crow often wore necklaces and other decorations made of bones, shells, beads, and porcupine quills.

Crow women made their families' clothing from animal skins. Men wore simple shirts and leggings with leather belts. They also wore earrings and necklaces made of bone or shell. For special occasions, they had beautiful clothes decorated with paint, beads, and porcupine quills. Their saddles, bridles, and horse blankets were covered with fancy designs. Women wore leggings and long dresses decorated with elk teeth. Both men and women wore soft leather shoes called moccasins. In the winter, they bundled up in buffalo-skin robes.

The Crow camped in cone-shaped tents called tepees. Tepees were made of buffalo skins stretched over long wooden poles. Women could put up or take down these tents quickly, whenever the tribe needed to move on. The walls of the tepee were often

Long wooden poles provided the frame for the buffalo skins that covered Crow tepees.

decorated with paintings of great warriors and hunters. At night, the family slept on mattresses made of animal hides. A carefully tended fire kept the tepee warm.

Each member of the tribe played an important role in its well-being. Fathers taught their sons to hunt and fight. Mothers taught their daughters how to prepare food, build and tear down tepees, and sew clothing.

Coupsticks

Each Crow band had its own chief. To become chief, a man had to prove himself by accomplishing four difficult tasks. He had to lead a successful raid against an enemy tribe. He had to capture an enemy's horses. Another task was to steal a weapon out of the hands of a live enemy. Finally,

he had to be the first member of a war party to get close enough to touch an enemy with a special stick called a **coupstick.**

Calling on the Spirits

The Crow believed that each tribe member had a **guardian** spirit who guided him or her through life. These spirits took the form of animals or objects in nature. They gave people wealth and happiness.

A young Crow man would go out alone on a vision quest.

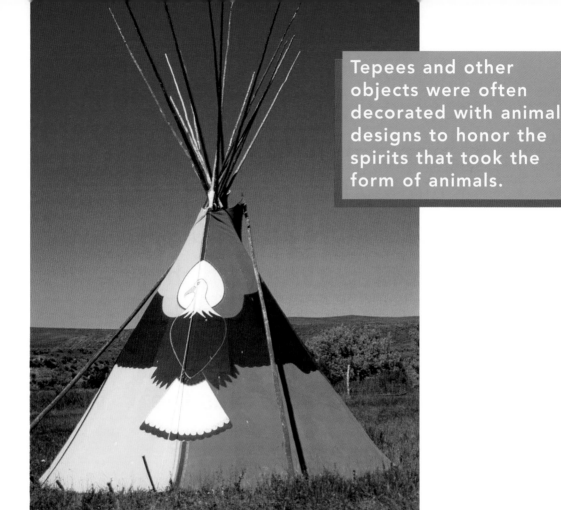

Tepees and other objects were often decorated with animal designs to honor the spirits that took the form of animals.

This was a time to connect with his guardian spirit and hear what the spirit might say to him. He would then gather sacred objects that were symbols of the power given to him by the guardian spirit. Those objects were put in medicine bundles, which tribe members kept for health and good luck.

The Sun Dance was the most important religious ceremony of all. It was held whenever a member of the tribe needed a vision, wanted power to heal a sick family member, or required strength to carry out revenge on his

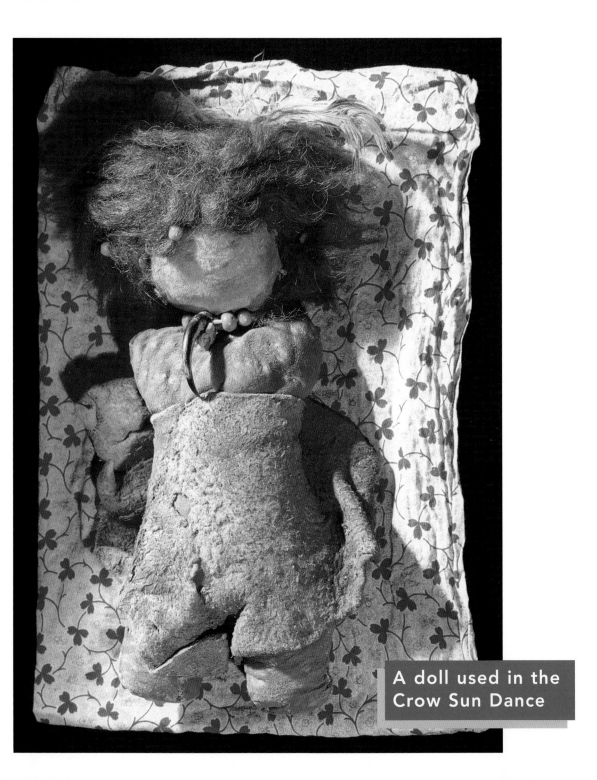

A doll used in the
Crow Sun Dance

enemies. He would ask for help from a shaman, or holy man. Other members of the tribe would join them. To prepare for the Sun Dance, they often went without food or sleep for days. Then they sang and danced and performed a complicated ceremony around a doll attached to a wheel or tree. They participated in painful tests to prove their courage and endurance. Tribe members also held ceremonies

Three Crow men pose outside a sweat lodge.

in sweat lodges. These buildings were dome-shaped huts heated with steam that was created when water was poured on hot stones.

A Crow man holds a pipe
used for smoking tobacco.

To the Crow, the tobacco plant was the most sacred object of all. It was the whole reason their tribe existed. Male members of the tribe smoked tobacco before leading war parties or making peace. Those who grew and cared for the plants were honored members of the Tobacco Society.

The End of the Old Way

In the early 1800s, President Thomas Jefferson sent a group of explorers to scout the land west of the Mississippi River. He wanted them to see if they could find a water route to link the Atlantic and Pacific oceans. Through the explorers' reports, America discovered all the wonders of the West.

Meriwether Lewis and William Clark explored the lands west of the Mississippi between 1804 and 1806. They traveled to the Pacific coast and back, meeting many American Indians along the way.

A wagon train heads west on the Oregon Trail in 1866.

Soon thousands of white **settlers** began moving across the Great Plains in search of land. Some claimed land and built their homes right in the middle of Crow territory. Others passed through the area as they made their way farther west. The settlers' wagon trains disturbed the migrating patterns of the buffalo. It became harder and harder for the Crow to find food. The natural environment that had supported them for so long was changed forever. Starvation as well as diseases carried by the settlers threatened to wipe out the tribe.

The Crow had to compete with other tribes for what was left of the land and its resources. Although they fought with the Lakota Sioux and the Nez Perce, the Crow tried to keep peace with the settlers. The Crow thought that if they could develop

A Crow warrior fighting for the U.S. Army rides into a Sioux camp.

good relationships with the U.S. Army, they would be protected from their enemies and receive better treatment from the government.

The Crow fought alongside the U.S. Army against other Indian tribes. They acted as scouts for Lieutenant Colonel George Armstrong Custer before his defeat at the Battle of the Little Bighorn in 1876.

Though the Crow cooperated with the U.S. Army, they were treated no differently than the other Indian tribes. Tribal leaders signed peace treaties at Fort Laramie in 1851 and 1868. They were forced to move their people onto a **reservation**.

A Man of Vision

Chief Plenty Coups (left) had a vision that convinced him the Crow must work with the U.S. government in order for his people to survive. In the late 1800s, he traveled to Washington, D.C., to represent the Crow and seek help from the government. He spoke out about the unfair treatment his people had often received. He became a skillful negotiator, learning how to get the attention of powerful government officials.

In 1921, this famous and powerful Crow chief was chosen to represent all American Indians at the dedication ceremony for the Tomb of the Unknown Soldier at Arlington National Cemetery.

The Crow Today

There are more than 10,000 Crow in the United States today. Most of them still live on or near the 2.2-million-acre Crow Indian reservation in south-central Montana. The reservation is rich in natural resources. Many Crow pursue careers in forestry, farming,

A Crow middle school student gets homework help from his mom.

Crow firefighters from Montana help fight a forest fire in New Mexico.

hunting, fishing, and mining. Some own businesses, including restaurants, hotels, campgrounds, and tourist attractions. Other members of the tribe work as doctors, lawyers, teachers, police officers, and social workers.

Every summer, thousands of people travel to the Little Bighorn Battlefield, where tribe members reenact the Battle of the Little Bighorn.

The Native American Memorial (below) at the Little Bighorn Battlefield honors the memory of the American Indians that died in the battle.

This is just one way the Crow remember their history. Many also gather at the Crow Powwow, Rodeo, and Race Meet in Hardin, Montana. At this festival, tribe members honor their heritage by dressing in traditional clothing and performing ceremonial songs and dances. Members compete in rodeo events and arrow-throw competitions, as well as newer entertainments such as golf and basketball tournaments.

A girl in traditional Crow dress

A Crow man talks to a young boy. Older members of the tribe work hard to make sure younger members understand the proud history of their people.

It is not just at annual events such as powwows that tribal history and **culture** are celebrated and passed on to younger generations. Newspapers, magazines, and Web sites help all members of the tribe keep up with Crow current events as well as learn more about the tribe's history. Moving forward while honoring the past, the Crow look eagerly toward the future of their proud people.

To Find Out More

Here are some additional resources to help you learn more about the Crow:

 **Books**

Goble, Paul. **Crow Chief: A Plains Indians Story.** Orchard Books, 1995.

Kavasch, E. Barrie. **Crow Children and Elders Talk Together.** Rosen Publishing Group, 2003.

Lassieur, Allison. **Apsaalooke (Crow) Nation.** Capstone Press, 2002

Ryan, Marla Felkins. **Crow.** Gale Group, 2002.

Tarbescu, Edith. **Crow.** Scholastic Library Publishing, 2000.

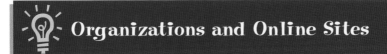

Organizations and Online Sites

Apsaalooke Nation
http://www.crownations.net

Visit this official Crow nation site to learn more about the tribe's history and government and to view pictures of Crow people in traditional dress.

National Museum of the American Indian
Fourth Street and Independence Avenue SW Washington, DC 20024 202-633-1000
http://www.nmai.si.edu/

Visit the museum to learn more about American Indian history and culture.

Red Shield and Running Wolf
http://www.indigenouspeople. net/redshiel.htm

You can read "Red Shield and Running Wolf" at this site containing Crow stories as well as tales from many other American Indian tribes.

Important Words

coupstick a wooden stick used by a warrior to demonstrate his courage

culture the way of life of a group of people

guardian someone who guards or protects something

negotiator one who discusses something in order to solve a problem or reach an agreement

nomadic moving from place to place

reservation an area of land set aside by the government as a place for American Indians to live

sacred holy; having to do with religion; something deserving of great respect

settler a person who makes a home in a new place

supernatural something that science and natural law cannot explain

Index

(**Boldface** page numbers indicate illustrations.)

Meet the Author

Christin Ditchfield is an author, conference speaker, and host of the nationally syndicated radio program *Take It to Heart!* Her articles have been featured in magazines all over the world. A former elementary school teacher, Christin has written more than thirty books for children on a wide range of topics, including sports, science, and history. She makes her home in Sarasota, Florida.